A Beginning-to-Read Book

Groundhog Day

by Mary Lindeen

NORWOOD HOUSE PRESS

DEAR CAREGIVER, The *Beginning to Read—Read and Discover* books provide emergent readers the opportunity to explore the world through nonfiction while building early reading skills. The text integrates both common sight words and content vocabulary. These key words are featured on lists provided at the back of the book to help your child expand his or her sight word recognition, which helps build reading fluency. The content words expand vocabulary and support comprehension.

Nonfiction text is any text that is factual. The Common Core State Standards call for an increase in the amount of informational text reading among students. The Standards aim to promote college and career readiness among students. Preparation for college and career endeavors requires proficiency in reading complex informational texts in a variety of content areas. You can help your child build a foundation by introducing nonfiction early. To further support the CCSS, you will find Reading Reinforcement activities at the back of the book that are aligned to these Standards.

Above all, the most important part of the reading experience is to have fun and enjoy it!

Sincerely,

Shannon Cannon

Shannon Cannon, Ph.D.
Literacy Consultant

Norwood House Press • P.O. Box 316598 • Chicago, Illinois 60631
For more information about Norwood House Press please visit our website at
www.norwoodhousepress.com or call 866-565-2900.
© 2016 Norwood House Press. Beginning-to-Read™ is a trademark of Norwood House Press.
All rights reserved. No part of this book may be reproduced or utilized in any form or by any
means without written permission from the publisher.

Editor: Judy Kentor Schmauss
Designer: Lindaanne Donohoe

Photo Credits:

Shutterstock, cover, 1, 4-5, 6, 8-9, 10-11, 12-13, 14-15, 18-19, 20-21, 22,
23 (Dainis Derics), 26-27 (Alan Freed), 28-29; Dreamstime, 7 (©Photawa),
16-17 (©Rabbitrabbit002), 24-25 (©Chillax33); iStock, 3

Library of Congress Cataloging-in-Publication Data
    Lindeen, Mary.
    Groundhog Day / by Mary Lindeen.
        pages cm. – (A beginning to read book)
    Summary: "Learn about where groundhogs live, what they eat, and their
    special role in Groundhog Day festivities. This title includes reading
    activities and a word list"– Provided by publisher.
    ISBN 978-1-59953-688-0 (library edition : alk. paper)
    ISBN 978-1-60357-773-1 (ebook)
    1. Groundhog Day–Juvenile literature. I. Title.
    GT4995.G76L56 2015
    394.261–dc23
                                        2014047633

Manufactured in the United States of America in Stevens Point, Wisconsin. 275N-062015

FEBRUARY 2

GROUNDHOG DAY

Groundhog Day is a special day.

It is always on the same date
in February.

This little animal is a groundhog.

It is part of the squirrel family.

Groundhogs can climb trees.

They can swim in the water, too.

But groundhogs live
in the ground.

Groundhogs eat grass and other plants.

They eat fruit and tree bark.

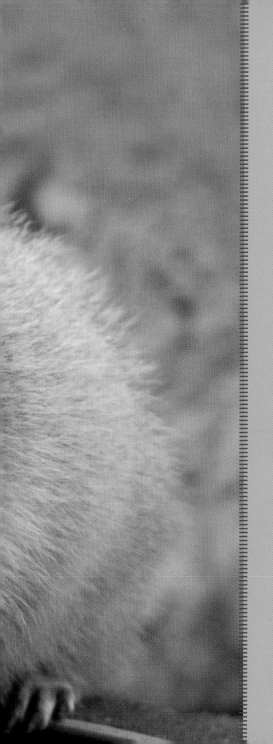

Groundhogs eat a lot in the summer.

They get very fat.

Groundhogs sleep all winter long.

They get up when spring comes.

Some people have a party on Groundhog Day.

They put on big hats.

They tell about Groundhog Day.

Then the groundhog
comes out.

It looks for its
shadow.

Does it see its shadow?

No?

Then spring will come soon.

Does it see its shadow?
Yes?

Then winter will last longer.

The groundhog goes back in.

The party is over.

Thank you,
groundhog.

You can go back
to sleep now.

See you next year!

...READING REINFORCEMENT...

CRAFT AND STRUCTURE

To check your child's understanding of this book, recreate the following diagram on a sheet of paper. Read the book with your child, and then help him or her fill in the diagram using what they learned. Work together to identify some of the cause-and-effect relationships in this book:

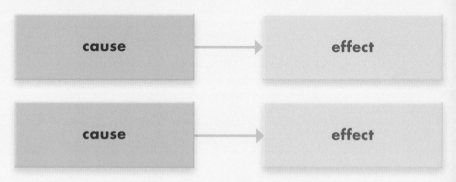

VOCABULARY: Learning Content Words

Content words are words that are specific to a particular topic. All of the content words for this book can be found on page 32. Use some or all of these content words to complete one or more of the following activities:

• Create a word web for one or more of the content words. Write the word itself in the center of the web, and synonyms (words with similar meanings), antonyms (words with opposite meanings), or other related words in the outer spokes.

• Say a content word. Have your child say the first word that comes to his or her mind. Discuss connections between the two words.

• Have your child find and cut out two magazine pictures that remind him or her of the meaning of each content word.

• Say a content word and have your child act out its meaning.

• Name one or two attributes of a content word without saying the word; for example, *This is made of paper and has words and pictures in it.* (book) Have your child guess the word. Switch roles.

FOUNDATIONAL SKILLS: Adjectives

Adjectives are words that describe nouns (people, places, things, and ideas); for example, *pretty*, *green*, and *four* are all adjectives. Have your child identify the words that are adjectives in the list below. Then help your child find adjectives in this book.

animal	special	little
big	longer	squirrel
climb	sleepy	fruit

CLOSE READING OF INFORMATIONAL TEXT

Close reading helps children comprehend text. It includes reading a text, discussing it with others, and answering questions about it. Use these questions to discuss this book with your child:

- Which animal family does a groundhog belong to?
- What are two things that all groundhogs have in common?
- Using what you know about groundhogs, what kind of home would you design for a groundhog?
- What do shadows have to do with Groundhog Day?
- What would happen if the groundhog didn't come out of his hole on Groundhog Day?
- Why do you think some people want to know when spring is coming?

FLUENCY

Fluency is the ability to read accurately with speed and expression. Help your child practice fluency by using one or more of the following activities:

- Reread this book to your child at least two times while he or she uses a finger to track each word as you read it.
- Read the first sentence aloud. Then have your child reread the sentence with you. Continue until you have finished this book.
- Ask your child to read aloud the words they know on each page of this book. (Your child will learn additional words with subsequent readings.)
- Have your child practice reading this book several times to improve accuracy, rate, and expression.

••• Word List •••

Groundhog Day uses the 79 words listed below. *High-frequency* words are those words that are used most often in the English language. They are sometimes referred to as sight words because children need to learn to recognize them automatically when they read. *Content words* are any words specific to a particular topic. Regular practice reading these words will enhance your child's ability to read with greater fluency and comprehension.

High-Frequency Words

a	does	long(er)	people	up
about	for	look(s)	put	very
all	get	next	same	water
always	go(es)	no	see	when
and	have	now	some	will
back	in	of	tell	you
big	is	on	the	year
but	it	other	then	
can	its	out	they	
come(s)	last	over	this	
day	little	part	too	

Content Words

animal	February	lot	soon	thank
bark	fruit	live	special	tree(s)
climb	grass	party	spring	winter
date	ground	plants	squirrel	yes
eat	groundhog(s)	shadow	summer	
family	hats	sleep	swim	

••• About the Author

Mary Lindeen is a writer, editor, parent, and former elementary school teacher. She has written more than 100 books for children and edited many more. She specializes in early literacy instruction and books for young readers, especially nonfiction.

••• About the Advisor

Dr. Shannon Cannon is a teacher educator in the School of Education at UC Davis, where she also earned her Ph.D. in Language, Literacy, and Culture. She serves on the clinical faculty, supervising pre-service teachers and teaching elementary methods courses in reading, effective teaching, and teacher action research.